# *How to Make Sense of Suffering*

Marguerite Duportal

# How to Make Sense of Suffering

SOPHIA INSTITUTE PRESS®
Manchester, New Hampshire

*How to Make Sense of Suffering* is a revised edition of *Bearing Your Troubles Well: Your Path to Peace in Difficult Times* (Manchester, New Hampshire: Sophia Institute Press, 1998), an abridged English translation of Marguerite Duportal's *De la Souffrance*. This edition uses the translation by Romauld Pecasse, published under the title *A Key to Happiness: The Art of Suffering* (Milwaukee: Bruce Publishing Company, 1944).



Cover design by Carolyn McKinney.

Printed in the United States of America.

Sophia Institute Press
Box 5284, Manchester, NH 03108
1-800-888-9344

www.SophiaInstitute.com



*Nihil obstat:* H. B. Ries, *Censor Librorum*
*Imprimatur:* Moses E. Kiley, Archbishop of Milwaukee
December 15, 1943

**Library of Congress Cataloging-in-Publication Data**

Duportal, Marguerite, b. 1869.
[De la souffrance. English]
Bearing your troubles well : your path to peace in difficult times / Marguerite Duportal.
p. cm.

"An abridged English translation of Marguerite Duportal's De la Souffrance. This 1998 edition by Sophia Institute Press uses the translation by Romauld Pecasse published under the title A Key to Happiness : the art of suffering (Milwaukee: Bruce Publishing Company, 1944)." — T.p. verso.
ISBN 0-918477-81-6 (pbk.)
1. Suffering — Religious aspects — Christianity. 2. Consolation. I. Title.

BT732.7.D8713 1998
231'.8 — dc21 98-34299 CIP

# Contents

# *How to Make Sense of Suffering*

# Introduction

Confronting myself with the obvious and unquestionable experience known as actual suffering, what invariably is my immediate reaction to it? Doubtless, it is a profound aversion. I dread the very thought of it. Even when impersonally considering the subject, should the menace of something painful suddenly obtrude itself, my first impulse would be to flee to avoid it, to resist its power.

Such is the instinct of my mind, the instinct of my whole being. But what will my afterthought, my second impulse, be?

Face-to-face with pain, my second thought is this: No matter what I may do, I cannot escape it. In fact, I see clearly that no one escapes it. Those who have flattered themselves most and boasted of their immunity, have at some time or other, perhaps frequently, come to realize rudely their illusion.

I know still further that here on earth, suffering is unequally distributed. But a secret and pitiless voice warns me that this inequality does not arise from man's cleverness or his awkwardness. Without doubt, there are evils that, according to the conduct of my life, I can either avoid or inevitably draw down upon my head. But there still remains that share of sorrow, unknown to me in kind and in degree, that I cannot evade. This share I must accept, making it my own without counting the cost, be it light or heavy. I have already felt something of it. I have suffered; I am suffering now; I shall suffer still more. This much is evident.

And what will be my second impulse? The first was to flee from suffering, to avoid it. I cannot do this, cannot carry it out. What, then, can be done?

Nothing else but to receive this undesired visitor, one to whom my door would never have been opened had he not entered unbidden. How shall I greet this guest whom I simply cannot welcome? What attitude shall I assume toward him? It is useless to close my eyes, to try to cast the intruder — this nuisance — out the window. I know it cannot be done. Better let me learn how to suffer, to suffer as well as possible and in the best way possible.

In fact, no other course remains. It is the one practical solution to the problem of suffering.

Note the facility with which words are used. "I bore my suffering well"; you constantly hear it said. But to suffer much is one thing; to suffer well is quite another. In suffering well, one suffers less than otherwise. There are a thousand ways of suffering at a disadvantage. How few persons, if they weighed their words properly, would have any right to say, "I have suffered well."

*Your temperament affects how you bear suffering*

Our suffering varies according to our character. The good or bad quality of our character influences the good or bad quality of our suffering. Our suffering corresponds to our temperament. Under the stress of pain, the apathetic become discouraged, the violent rebel, and the envious become morbid or evil-minded. The meek, the generous, the humble, and the zealous whose zeal is noble suffer "with a good heart." Suffering with a good heart brings the least bitterness into our pains, and is least productive of new sufferings.

Badly disposed characters undergo suffering in a way that intensifies ill-humor in themselves and inflicts the reactions of their trials upon others. Some scapegoat is necessary for them. By this we do not mean a victim to be tortured at will, but someone on whom to thrust the weight of the suffering endured. But does that lighten their burden? Not in the least! Pain cannot be transmitted like a package to anyone else. Those who try to spread it out only increase it. So a new suffering is created, and the infliction of it augments their own.

*Even amid sufferings you must carry out your duties*
Indeed, under all circumstances, a good temperament is a most valuable ally, helpful above all in times of misfortune. It lessens the keenness of the pangs of sorrow, sets limits to their depressing influence, extends and radiates the healing properties of affliction, and permits — as well as, if not better than, before — the fulfillment of what we call duty. For duty will never disappear from our lives.

When misfortune befalls us, whether as a visible catastrophe or as a tragedy that is locked up within our secret heart, draining its last drop of blood without anyone else suspecting it, we cannot afford to bury ourselves in our despair. We cannot afford to reject all participation in the ceaselessly pulsating life around us in order to permit our thought to concentrate on only one point, forgetting and disregarding everything else. Willy-nilly, the law of self-preservation quickly reasserts itself. Our responsibilities compel us to face moral and physical exigencies of every kind, to resume urgent occupations, and to meet persons toward whom we have assumed obligations. For certain natures, this compulsory resumption of exterior activities is a blessing, a fruit of suffering, a relief in the trial; for others, it is a new trial. For all, it is the beginning of a new life.

All these things must be done; we did them in a happy mood before the affliction came; we must do them now while suffering, even if we should feel ourselves unhappy. We cannot escape them. Hard hit though one may be, he retains his role, his mission, and his place in the economy of the universe; he remains himself; he remains a member of the human society, a creature of God. Therefore the issue is to know how to bear sorrow in the presence of God, in the presence of our fellow men, and within oneself.

Chapter
One

# *Understand why God allows suffering*

∞

To suffer in the presence of God! Whether we have reflected on this or not, it remains a fact, solemn as the thought undoubtedly is. "It makes one tremble to write in the presence of the Blessed Trinity," says Ernest Psichari. Well may we tremble while considering that we are compelled to bear our heavy and blessed burden of sorrow in the presence of the Father who created us, of the Son who redeemed us, and of the Holy Spirit who showers His grace upon us.

∞

*God has concern for your sufferings*

But no! Let us not tremble. Let us rather expand our wounded heart. God sees me suffer: what solace! God knows the history of my woes, even down to the most intimate detail: what a consolation!

To tell one's tale of woe must offer great relief, because we nearly always see the afflicted seeking obligingly charitable persons who are willing to lend patient ears to the minute recitation of their misfortunes. But we need not trouble God about this. He is well informed. He knows all, not only because He sees all and recognizes all, but also because He ordains and allots our suffering.

This statement should neither shock nor scandalize us. It is a part of the teaching of the Church and gives to pain a sacred character. If we suffer, it is not by chance or by accident. *Chance* and *accident* are empty words; they are void of sense, conventional expressions that cannot be defined or analyzed. If we suffer, it is because God permits or wills it.

Ah, yes! Poor soul! Disconsolate over the death of one most dear to you: God wanted this heartbreaking separation; God did want to sever these intimate ties without which you seem to be unable to live. And yes, unfortunate creature, doomed to the miseries of poverty or to the tortures of disease: God did want you to have this agony, this illness, and these sufferings. Yes, even to you, dear soul, the target of undeserved malice, discouraging failures, and adversities of every kind.

Far from being disinterested in all of this, as if He were but a heedless or indifferent guardian, God wanted it all.

*Sin brought suffering into the world*

Without doubt, He did not write this beforehand into the initial plan of creation, which was the work of absolute goodness. But that this work might attain the highest perfection, He permitted the existence of our moral liberty. And since this moral liberty, without which we should be mere puppets, was through Adam applied by humanity in the manner known to us all, and since the ransom to be consequently offered for fallen man — a new work of absolute goodness — demanded reparation, suffering entered into the world.

The pure and simple play of secondary causes is often advanced in order to explain the tragic accidents and catastrophes that desolate our planet; namely, the free will of man or the inexorable evolution of natural phenomena is alleged. But God is the source of both the natural and the supernatural. Secondary causes revert to the first causes which He has established. He has foreseen and allowed all their repercussions in establishing them.

These repercussions cannot in any way have fatal consequences that might elude God's omniscience, nor are they such that God might be compelled to permit their occurrence beyond His direction or correction. Rather, the contrary is so. As an inventor, master of his machine, adjusts its wheels at will in order to make them operate uninterruptedly in the original plan of his work, so, too, God — whose action is as necessary for the conservation of the world as it was in its creation out of nothing — knows and can modify according to His will the conditions natural for the evolution of facts, material accidents, and human actions. He knows this and can do it without having constant recourse to miracles, which means without a violent reversal of the laws He has created and established, and without departing from His immutability; for He sees all in the eternal view with which He regards the past, the present, and the future as ever spread out before Him, and conformably with which He controls all things.

Were it not so, what would be the purpose of prayer, this instinctive and ineradicable surging of the heart and mind? Prayer would be neither natural nor reasonable, if it had no efficacy, or if this efficacy were totally incompatible either with the implacability of blind forces abandoned to themselves or the operation of individual wills over which the sovereign will of God would have no way of regaining possession.

*God can bring good out of evil*

According to His good pleasure, God can correct and repair, case by case, the evil effects that our vitiated will and the fallen state of everything around us bring on — effects always disastrous to the ultimate good, which is His goal. He has proved this in a marvelous way by the Redemption. In that blessed moment of time, God made use of His Son to supply the infinite means necessary for the redemption of humanity. He also employs the cooperation and acquiescence of each individual human creature, throughout the course of the centuries, to promote its own freely willed personal advance.

"God wished to give the dignity of causes to His creatures," says St. Thomas.[1] Thus an adult wishing to give a small child the pleasure of personally mailing a letter takes him into his arms and raises it to the height of the mailbox. Evidently it is the adult who actually sends the letter deposited by the child. So, too, God remains the absolute master to whom all contingencies

[1] St. Thomas Aquinas (1225-1274), Dominican philosopher and theologian.

defer. All acts for which man is responsible, although they be free in their execution, remain subject to God in their results. "Man plants the cause today; God ripens the effects tomorrow," said Victor Hugo.[2] In the words of Joan of Arc,[3] "The arms of men will fight the battle, but it is God who will grant the victory."

God employs the human will as a secondary cause. When this will is good, He blesses it by blessing its works. He reproves the will that is evil, leaving to it the full responsibility for the wrong it does, while His Providence is able to convert this into a blessing.

Inextricable to our understanding, this maze, this interweaving of all contingencies, causes, and effects, is for God merely ample yet magnificent ramification of all that lives and throbs in the luminous center of Truth and Love. All is repaired by love; everything dissolves itself in love. God wants and does all things for the best. He ordains everything that happens, except sin. God allows the commission of sin, because He respects the free will of man which He created; but He forcibly subjects it to His domination by the punishment that follows sin

[2] Victor Hugo (1802-1885), novelist and playwright.

[3] St. Joan of Arc (1412-1431), French heroine.

sooner or later, because He is the Supreme Power and Infinite Justice.

∞

*Suffering can correct, cure, and strengthen you*

Therefore God wants the sufferings of the human race, as a physician wants the privations and pains of a patient in order to cure him, or possibly, so that individuals may be aided to reach a higher perfection through it.

In fact, humanity is ill. It suffers under an incoherence of judgment, depravity of desires, and systemic anemia. It needs a strong, expert hand to correct, cure, and strengthen it. Not depraved in its nature, but weakened and impaired by the Fall, it must be corrected, trained, and elevated.

At times, God chastises us because we are guilty, and again He seeks to stimulate within us a new vigor, to test and try us out, so that we may make further progress. Sometimes He treats us as favored children, by depriving us of an illusory or mediocre good, in order to give or preserve one that is incomparably superior. Thus He may wrest from our hands a dangerous object, whose hurtfulness our own eager imprudence did not perceive; or He may strip us of the best of human things, in order to make us cling with greater force and intensity to the supernatural, to the divine joys of His love, in perfect and happy detachment from all else.

This is what I discover in my sorrows through logic, and not through logic only, but also by experience. Why, then, should I rebel? And why should I murmur?

How can I guess into which category God places me when He strikes me? What shall I think when I see misfortune befall my neighbors? Are they privileged friends of God or culprits whom He is punishing? How can I know whether I am being punished or loved or merely put to a test, when I myself am exposed to the blows of misfortune?

I shall have the answer, if I reflect a little and examine myself with great sincerity. My first step is to avoid passing formal judgment on anything that concerns my neighbor. It is not for me to know whether this individual has personally deserved punishment or reward. Moreover, how can I know the intimate responsibilities, the hidden failings, and the secrets of heroism in the soul of any person? The department of public safety itself has serious difficulties in trying to protect society against the fomenters of disturbance in the established order. If the individual in his private life has a legal claim to protection against prying investigations, how much more inviolable in fact and in law should be the realm of conscience.

Let us, therefore, leave the affair of judging others to God. It is simply none of our business. What is important for us is to look at our own particular case, to reflect upon it and study it.

### *You must learn to see God's loving hand even in your suffering*

And here let me examine myself. A child punished by his parents for serious disobedience has not the least doubt as to the reason for his punishment. Why, then, when I am that child before God, am I not equally conscious of my transgressions?

During maneuvers, a soldier knows perfectly well that the ambuscades and obstacles to be overcome are purposely planned by the officers in command. They are to teach him how to achieve victory, how to triumph. When I am this soldier, am I at the same time making myself fit?

When a devoted father takes from the hands of his child the knife with which the child is playing, lest the child wound himself, or snatches the bottle of poison the child is raising to his lips; when he calls a surgeon to excise a gangrenous member, lest it infect the whole body, does not this father pour out the full measure of his tenderness and give infallible proof of his passionate desire for the welfare of his child? Will not the child, once he has attained the use of reason, be the first to thank him? Am I less intelligent, less grateful than this child?

You who love God, who pray to Him, and who are His friends; you who do good and wish no evil; you who share your bread with the poor and seek only the happiness of your fellow man; you the upright, the good, the loyal servants, who suddenly see your whole life ruined by one of those frightful shocks under which at the first moment even the courageous give way; you who imperceptibly are subject, little by little and yet with relentless persistence to repudiations that pierce you to the quick, more than anyone else suspects: be sure that your welfare depends upon these very conditions! I mean your eternal welfare, and possibly also your temporal well-being. God, who at times punishes in this world, at times also makes recompense in this world. He converts a great impending or even merely threatening evil into a signal benefit. That which He took away from you, even though it rent your heart, possibly prevented the granting of the exquisite gift He had in store for you during your earthly days; it certainly interfered with that which He wishes to give you at its best in the next world.

Moreover, all, even the purest, need to be purified still more; and all, even the strongest, must be still more strengthened.

∞

### *Rebelling against suffering is foolish and futile*

Truly, therefore, there is nothing illogical, and consequently nothing revolting in my affliction. Away with the thought of rebellion! Not only is it unjust; it is useless and bootless. Of all the attitudes assumed in regard to suffering, it is the most absurd. *Why should I rebel, O Lord?* What good is there in rebelling against a power more crushing than a millstone falling upon an ant?

And we shall not find the least alleviation in our suffering by rebelling. It is not by rebelling that we acquire the art of suffering. Rebels against rightly established and functioning authorities are certainly not artists; they are vandals. Kicking and stamping does not bring us a step forward. To dash the head against the wall is worse than senseless. Only the brute may enter into blind and impotent rage upon losing its prey, when it is wounded or made captive.

The soul of man has other resources. Or rather, it has only one: to adopt an attitude that corresponds with the divine intention; to allow God to guide it whither He will, along the path He assigns.

Stripped and crushed though we may be, let us remain gratefully submissive to Him who crushes and strips us. If He does this to us, it is within His right to do so. It is, I almost dare to say, His duty to do so. The full explanation of sorrow will be given to us only in Heaven. What we know of it here on earth is sufficient for everyone who reasons honestly and in good faith.

After all, God is not a dry-eyed torturer, an unfeeling witness of the pain He inflicts upon His creatures. Pity, the divine pity that moves His fatherly heart, seeks only to flow down upon us, if we but wish to raise our docile and confident eyes toward Him. No surgeon ever cleans and binds with greater solicitude the painful incisions that he has made on the patient he desires to save than does God in soothing and healing our pains when we consent to allow Him to do so.

Oh, the overflowing and tender pity of God! If we only knew how to entrust ourselves to Thee, how refreshing to the poignant wounds of our soul would be the melting of Thy tenderness.

But to experience these benefits, one must believe in this tenderness, despite conflicting appearances. One must believe in this God of mercy, who shields us while putting us under trial; in this God who is the living and infinite miracle of goodness. We must believe in Him, because He exists, a fact proved by everything about us. And again, if one does not believe, there will be nothing left but for us to give to this restless world the definition coined by I know not what humorist: "The work of the Devil gone mad."

Chapter
Two

# Trust in God's loving plan

Still, numerous complaints flow from our lips. In many a conscience, half-suppressed protestations murmuringly assert themselves. It would be unfair to remain silent and give no answer to the objections made by these souls to the justification of suffering.

Let us remark, first of all, that very seldom does one hear happy people criticize the order of the world. In his naive egoism, the happy man is astonished even at the thought that some people are dissatisfied. Jules Sandeau remarks that the Marquis de la Seiglière, sitting comfortably at a large window facing his spacious park, made this unsavory and unconsciously cruel reflection: "Imagine! Some people actually complain against life." Yet the so-called happy man who looks around a little will see some people who suffer. Even if he does not take the trouble to do so, willingly or not, he hears the cries of the multitude, and feels the repercussions of lives less happy than his own. He becomes conscious of this only when these manifestations begin to threaten the peace and felicity of his own selfish existence. Then, and then only, does he begin to assume that the world is poorly fashioned and that God might have made it differently. Let misfortune befall him, and forthwith he becomes enraged, turns cynic, becomes a person to whom God is only a myth and a monster.

The philosophy that changes according to the manner in which one is affected by the calamities that course over our planet does not merit the name *philosophy*. It is not even a token of intelligence.

The misfortune that suddenly leads to atheism or drives to blasphemy is never given serious thought as long as it concerns only a neighbor. When such ills befall others, no one thinks of denying the existence of God or of charging Him with cruelty. All that is said is, "Poor people! What a pity!" That's all! Secretly we flatter ourselves at our own better fortune. If we happen to be in a generous mood, we thank Heaven for having spared us and offer more or less platonic consolation to the victims.

It never strikes us that these victims might contradict the idea one continues to hold of the world as being a harmonious universe directed with wisdom and most agreeable to live in.

# Trust in God's loving plan

*Suffering must not shake your faith*

To lose faith because we have suffered, because we have been afflicted with some great pain, is to prove ourselves completely and astoundingly egotistic, and absolutely illogical. Recriminations arising from such a spirit are to be utterly disregarded.

We must now answer the objections and the doubts of honest souls, whether personally afflicted or not, who are disturbed by the law of suffering and who demand an explanation that will reconcile it, if not with God's justice, at least with His goodness, and at any rate with His omnipotence. Souls are not rarely found who, while trying to accept, to adore, and to submit, nevertheless do not succeed in silencing within themselves the instinct to rebel secretly against the author of so imperfect a world.

Their first objection is that it was within the power of God not to create us. Having created us, it is within His power to make us immune to suffering; and if suffering is the consequence of sin, it was within His power to make us incapable of sinning. In any case, it was within His power not to make all humanity share in the sin of the first man. Finally, He could have redeemed the human race by a single word, a look — if need be, with a single drop of the blood of Christ, without inaugurating this dolorous system of redemption through the tortures and death of the God-Man, together with the inevitableness of our own personal suffering.

Let us take up these objections in order.

### *God made you to share His gifts*

In the first place, it was within the power of God to leave us uncreated. Can anyone claim that this would have been better? Will anyone hold that while possessing within Himself countless riches and an abundance of gifts ready to satisfy any flood of desires He need only set in motion, God would have shown Himself more generous, more charitable, by keeping these treasures locked up within His bosom? Even to this, some may answer, "Yes, because He knew beforehand that these treasures would be shared only on very hard conditions. Therefore, it would have been better to leave us ignorant of life and its joys than to open to us the field of its sorrows."

But arguing thus, all human parents who bring children into the world commit a reprehensible act. Which father, which mother can say with certainty, "I will shield my child against even the slightest pain"? The moment a child enters this world, he commences to weep and cry. Without calling the parents tyrants, we see them smile, overjoyed at his cries and tears, which announce the commencement of life. The tenderest, most resolute, and considerate parents are precisely those who raise their child for his grand future by means of trials and exercises that are never without pain.

*It is your freedom that allows you to sin*

"Granted," some will answer, "but God could have created us immune to suffering. And if God has not created pain, if He has not created death, if these are only the frightful consequences of sin, then He should have created us impeccable."

Impeccable? And be nothing more than rational creatures that have received life without receiving either reason or liberty?

To say that we deplore this absence of impeccability is to claim that we prefer to be no more than a mere thing or a brute. But to be justly proud of our noble title of free and intelligent creatures, we must with equal necessity admit the obligation of tests and the indispensable freedom of choice. In order to grant us a conscious and meritorious impeccability, it was absolutely necessary to attribute to us the possibility of corruption and degeneracy; it was necessary to leave us free to degrade ourselves.

"We are prepared to admit that, too," says another, "but why should the Fall of the first man, succumbing to the first temptation, entail the condemnation of the whole human race? Why should the posterity of Adam and Eve bear the weight of their fault, a fault not one of us has personally committed, and for which we are chastised by falling under the lash of the general and inexorable law of suffering?"

The general and inexorable law of suffering to which all are subject is indeed a consequence of the sin of Adam and Eve. God willed that their erstwhile immunity to suffering should be lost by them, even while He forgave them. If they had not been forgiven, Hell would have closed over them as it did upon the fallen angels. The divine condescension has commuted this terrible punishment into a temporary expiation, to which the merits of the Redemption by Christ impart a superabundant reparative power.

*Everyone shares in expiation for sin*

We share in this temporary expiation for two reasons. First, born of tainted parents, we, too, are tainted. In fact, it is by inheritance that the Original Sin transmits itself and thus defiles the entire human nature. True, the individual human soul is not generated by the soul of ancestors. It is always created directly by God, intact and immortal. But on becoming wedded to body, to which, from the moment of conception, it becomes united and to which it adapts itself to the intimate communication, it also contracts its defilement. Henceforth, the perfection with which it was invested is lost. The Divine Artist, whose masterpiece it was, no longer recognizes it as His child. In order to restore its lost beauty, it will become necessary for the Creator Himself to descend to a most unexpected procedure of reparation and rehabilitation.

The second reason we share in the expiation of the first two sinners of the human race is that we all share in their culpability as soon as we begin to exist and to act by ourselves. The best among us falls seven times a day; and the worst criminal, through his own penitential acts, profits by the pardon merited by the Redeemer.

Only an unrepented personal crime can lead us into Hell. No one will be condemned to the pains of Hell on account of the sin of Adam and Eve.

It is evident that it was not the plan of the Creator to give us the joys of an eternal Heaven without having merited them. If human nature had not been jeopardized at its very root, we would have been born pure and endowed with grace, as were the first man and the first woman when they came from the hand of the Creator. Not improbably, every one of us would have been subjected to some trial, similar to that given our first parents. And who can say that he would have certainly triumphed in it?

Hence, since we all are tainted in our very birth, all more or less individually culpable in our personal lives, we must all share to a certain extent in the expiation of the sins of humanity, even as we all share in the redemption through Christ of this fallen, uplifted humanity, everlastingly relapsing, always able to rise again.

*Christ has suffered everything you suffer*

And now for the final argument: "But this redemption through Christ could have been accomplished without tortures on His part. A single sigh of the Messiah, being a sigh of God, would have sufficed to save the world and atone for the outrage committed against His infinite majesty. Why, then, the manger and its abasement? Why Golgotha with its opprobrium and tortures? Why the thirty-three years of self-sacrificing, painful, sorrowful life on which we at all costs, in part, must model our own life, if we wish to share in the fruits of redemption?"

No doubt, while imposing a temporary expiation upon us, the Man-God could have redeemed us by a sigh of His heart without condemning Himself to experience that cruel agony for us — suffering with us, like us, and far more than we ever can. If He had declined, however, to undergo these sufferings — which as God He had every right to do — what blasphemies might have been hurled against Him! The infidels would cry out, "Ah! God is mocking rejected mankind. He leaves men to their weakness, their struggles, their trials, their heartbreaks, while He remains enthroned in His impassive eternity, immovable and serene."

Meanwhile, amid this ranting of the impious, the humble and submissive would be nobly accepting their lot of provisional misery. We should then witness the strange, in a certain sense monstrous, fact that little, imperfect, sinful human beings would possess virtues that even the Man-God would not have practiced — heroic resignation, the spirit of sacrifice, and the immolation of self even unto death.

But "the Word was made flesh and dwelt amongst us."[4] With this the blasphemer is silenced and the believer pours out his love and gratitude. God Himself has come in person to share our punishment. He has taken our burden upon His shoulders, He has preceded us along the way of brambles and thorns. Having become man like ourselves, He has given us an example of patience, of self-abnegation, of courage, lest anyone ever dare to say that He wanted to ignore our afflictions and that we cannot bear them.

*God's plan has nobility, order, and beauty*

We have seen the least guilty, treading in the footsteps of the divine trainer of souls, become the most penitent. The whole world, astonished and thrilled to admiration, witnesses acts of sublime morality and of such exalted heroism as was unknown to the ancient world: the

[4] John 1:14.

mortification of the ascetics, the endurance of the martyrs, the charity of the saints, the love of the cross, the pardon of injuries. Who should dare to claim that if all this had been denied to the world, the world would not have lost the greater share of its beauty? Banish suffering and with it the valor that the noblest of human beings have cultivated while enduring it; banish their devotion while soothing the sufferings of others: then tell me if everything does not suddenly grow pale around you, in you, in Heaven and on earth.

Search wherever you may; try to imagine anything that God could or could not have made or fashioned differently; we shall never rise above the ideas traced according to His sovereign law, which necessarily must be our own law, because the created law derives from the creating law, and our concept of justice and right is only the reflection of the justice and righteousness of God.

Could another world built on concepts unknown to us, and better than the worlds we know, have been created by God? Certainly. To deny this would be to say that God, in creating this universe, had expended the full measure of His power, exhausted it, and once and for all had done His utmost. But God does not exhaust Himself. No matter what finite things He gives, He never gives in the fullest measure; whatever God may make, He can make it larger and better than it is. At the same time, we must declare that each one of His works taken by itself is perfectly beautiful and good. In this sense, God, being infinite, can always surpass Himself. Being perfect, He can produce only that which has perfect order and perfect beauty. The universe of which we form a part has been constructed on a magnificent plan, and was remodeled after its ruin — which was our work — on a plan still more admirable. In fact, the plan of redemption includes two inestimable favors: one retained for fallen humanity, the other granted to it. They are the precious prerogative of free will, which was not nullified by Original Sin; and the favor that infants, dying after Baptism, share through the intervention of the Church in the merits of the Savior and are admitted to eternal happiness without the necessity of gaining it by personal trial or effort.

Adore and lovingly kiss the hand of God, which twice has been extended to us in limitless liberality. Let us expand our soul under the eye of God, who is the light of our conscience, the reason of our reason, the judge of our justice, and the only enduring balm that soothes our anxiety.

Chapter
Three

# Find strength in union with God

Therefore, let not the saddened soul reject the hand of God, nor avoid His ineffable gaze. The soul will not feel compelled to avoid the countenance of God, even though it may add remorse to its sorrow. God's eye is intolerable only to the soul that remains obstinate in error. The very moment the soul breaks with this, it can lift its brow and seek the visage of its judge. At any rate, whether one wishes or not, God sees us; we cannot escape. "Adam, Adam, where art thou?"[5] is the word of Jehovah in Eden on the evening of the first sin, and the trembling sinner is obliged to appear before his angered Creator.

Why should not the humiliated, perplexed, but repentant soul dare to seek the countenance of God? If its faults made it worthy of contempt, its sufferings and concomitant regrets rehabilitate it. The sorrow of a soul, whether it has remained in the grace of God or has

[5] Cf. Gen. 3:9.

been reconciled with Him, is never unbearable. Nay more, it can become an unspeakable joy.

As soon as we rest in this thought: "I am at peace with God," an inexpressible solace arises within our hearts. Therefore, the first condition to suffer well and consequently to suffer less is to bear afflictions with a very pure conscience.

### *Peace with God can make suffering sweet*

"I am at peace with God." To be deeply imbued with this thought fills one with happiness in the midst of the greatest adversities. If one were at war with the rest of the world, with self, and with human passions, which are the fiercest enemies one can have, and at the same time were at peace with God, he would sail onward, resolutely, serenely, and joyously. It was the enchantment of this peace that made the martyrs exult in the midst of their tortures and encircled the brows of the victims with a heavenly radiance in the presence of their persecutors. Deprived of this peace, what joy can one know? What satisfaction can one feel? A troubled joy is a joy no longer, and a bad conscience knows no undisturbed joy. On the other hand, no irksomeness enters into the suffering of a good conscience, and suffering immune against worry hardly remains a suffering.

To be at peace with God is to find oneself immersed in an atmosphere, the slightest breath of which necessarily conveys sensation of life, while at the same time an admirably serene tranquillity takes possession of the soul. One can then no longer tell whether it is the sweetness of this peace that nourishes the sorrow or whether sorrow has melted away into sweetness.

But peace is not the final word in our relations with God, relations that are strengthened rather than broken by suffering. The saddened soul no longer contents itself with merely tasting the thought "I am at peace with God." It will amplify it with the necessary complement so prolific in the development of joy — namely, "I am united with God."

### *Union with God is the sum of all happiness*

Union with God! It is the immediate fruit and happy consequence of peace with God. The moment we are no longer against God, we are with Him. The instant we cease being rebels, we become friends, His chosen children. Union with God! It is the only, the full happiness for which we are created. It is the sum of all happiness and replaces everything. United with God, we associate ourselves with all that is good, beautiful, and precious. In God we find all that we might have lost, all that we could have possibly desired without ever attaining. No doubt about this. Nothing exists by itself. All existence is borrowed from God. Everything derives from God. Everything was made by Him, "and without Him was made nothing that was made."[6] The creatures we so admire, the things that please us, draw all their beauty, intelligence, and charm only from God. He is the source from which they emanate, and at the source, waters are purer and flow more abundantly than in the brooks, which become tainted in their course.

The moment we mention goodness, bliss, or favor, we speak of God. He is the author, the possessor, the distributor, and the hidden receiver *par excellence*. In God we associate ourselves with all goodness, perfect happiness, and every blessing, placed as it were into a container out of which nothing can fall.

But again I hear an objection and the expression of resentment: "Do we actually recover the tangible and

[6] John 1:3.

material things in God, things we have once lost, things our nature relished and enjoyed legitimately when used in conformity with the law instituted by the Creator Himself? For instance, do we recover our lost fortune or our physical health? Do we revive the sensible feeling of affection for objects that have been taken from us? How, then, can we affirm that we never lose anything if we live in constant union with God?"

St. Thomas teaches that persons deprived of certain purely terrestrial and material things here on earth, things that will not exist in the better world, can, at God's pleasure, know and possess them in a spiritual manner in the bliss of Heaven. On their behalf, God can transform these earthly and sensible joys in harmony with the intangible, the invisible, and the infinite. Heavenly bliss cannot be inferior to the happiness of this world, and in the perfect union with God, which will be completed only in Heaven, the human being will be spiritualized in such manner that the very essence of all created goodness can be communicated to him, even if the material substance in which this goodness was manifest no longer exists.

Something similar takes place here below when we try to spiritualize ourselves, that is, when we seek to unite ourselves with God as closely as possible. In Him we find all the harmonies of the most human joys transformed, transfigured.

### *We are torn between the things of Heaven and the things of earth*

To be so spiritualized costs considerable effort for man, composed, as he is, of elements that draw him downward as well as elements that beckon him upward. We are drawn downward not only by the perverted and vitiated part of our nature, but also by the simple fact that we are creatures formed of the "slime of the earth."[7] We are drawn downward by the attraction exerted upon us by the sensible and material world of which we are a part, by objects we can see, hear, and feel; by the human happiness for which we are made, not primarily, but incidentally; and finally because we bear within ourselves a homesickness for the paradise of Heaven and a homesickness for the paradise of Eden. We try in vain to convince ourselves that the most beautiful and the best creatures present to our eyes only a reflection of the

[7] Gen. 2:7.

goodness and beauty of God. We admit that ordinarily the thing we relish most keenly, to which we submit most willingly, is a reflected enchantment.

Original Sin is one excuse for this deviation of the lawful tendencies of our heart; but the mysterious state, the hidden life that envelops us in our relation with God is another. Even our Creator and Master, in commanding us to love Him above all things, does not require that we feel toward Him in the *emotional* center of our soul a love higher than that which we feel for most dearly beloved parents and most cherished friends. If that ever should happen to us, bless Him, for then we shall have found Heaven on earth. Let us not, however, be surprised, if ordinarily, the opposite happens. Nor should we feel guilty at this, provided we sustain toward God a preferential love, born of the disposition to sacrifice everything rather than offend Him.

### *You can be happy even in suffering*

To be sure, it is not a question of denying the existence of suffering and, in particular, physical suffering. We are not Stoics, nor do we say, "*Non dolet*" ("It does not hurt"). But we Christians do say that while enduring sufferings, and suffering keenly, we can be sincerely happy. We affirm the coexistence of sorrow and joy in the soul. We maintain that the idea is superior to sensation, and it is through the idea that accompanies our sufferings that these become either intolerable or tolerable and sweet. What renders Hell so terrible is that the damned are constrained to gnaw forever on the one idea that they have lost God. When, on the other hand, in this life, the idea of an adorable intimacy with Supreme Intelligence, with Sovereign Goodness, becomes operative and is welded to the sensation of corporal torment, this pain is alleviated to the extent of the preference given to things more sublime over those less so.

We shall be more or less happy in our daily lives, according to the habit we form of living for our lower or for our nobler selves, for matter or for spirit, for the senses or for an idea. We always suffer in inverse proportion to the intensity of the vital influence exercised by the idea within us. However, this idea must be Christian, because the idea of annihilation,[8] for instance, or

[8] The theory of annihilationism says that immortality is not a necessary attribute of the soul, but is conditional on the soul's behavior during its life in the body.

any other idea contrary to Catholic hope, far from attenuating affliction, rather augments it with all the intensity allowed the mind to give to it.

Tell me not that the idea of annihilation is bearable, that one can even find in it at least a reason for enduring the pains of life. If you deny heavenly life and the immortality of the soul, you will not, you cannot, actually derive from this negation the least efficacious consolation, the least courage to bear your ills. The courage that you might have or that you imagine to be derived from this wholly materialistic idea of annihilation, you derive precisely from the very care you take to banish this idea from your daily life. If you incessantly thought that the goal toward which you are proceeding is death, the complete destruction of your being; that none of your frustrated aspirations, none of your unsatisfied desires, shall be gratified; that no injustice will ever be requited, no misery ever banished, no affection perpetuated, then you either plunge into the deep abyss of the blackest marasmus, or you begin to live as the most cynical and brutal debauchee.

After all, there is no such thing as true indifference. What we call indifference is really the choice of something good that we sense to be superior to something else. Do you prefer honor to money? A good conscience to a profitable deal? The life of a friend to your own? The very choice itself is only the unconscious admission of the superiority of the spiritual over the material, and consequently implies the intrinsic condemnation of the idea of annihilation, because, although we have been witnesses of the decay of the body, we never have attended the death of a soul.

*God sustains you in your troubles*

To turn away from God in misfortune is to bring upon oneself harm a thousand times more cruel than that under which one thinks himself to be suffering. It is to reject at once all the sweetness and all the nobility of suffering. Let no one say, "It is nobler, grander to suffer alone, to suffer without support or consolation. My pride forbids me to depend upon God, to implore His pity on my plight, to bend my knee, and above all, to kiss the hand that strikes me."

Poor human pride! By what prodigy will you remain unbent, haughty like a statue? The human heart is made of flesh, not of stone. It is vain to pretend such obstinacy. In the secret of a lonely night, in the shadows of your own hushed home, or possibly those of a deserted chapel, someday you will sink on your knees, holding your swaying head in your hands, your eyes moistened and your pride conquered.

You cannot escape indefinitely. The need of an outstretched helping hand will be greater than your pretended spurning of sympathy. It is the hand of God you will seek to grasp, because you will then have learned only too well that the hand of man is elusive or heavy, and that in it your weakness will look in vain for sufficient support or your sensitiveness for a sufficiently delicate touch.

You who suffer: suffer close to God, as closely as possible. Whatever the nature or the intensity of your affliction, whatever the difficulty it presents, bear it in the presence of God. You will then, consciously and voluntarily, allow the penetration of divine care into all that you endure, no matter what happens without your wish or knowledge. You will then experience a kind of miracle taking place within yourself. Your formerly complicated sorrow will become simple, trouble will clarify itself, and the disproportionate will adjust itself to your strength. With ardent and unfaltering devotion, you will hold strictly to the decree of Providence. You will submit to it with reverence, with love, and with a sort of subdued jubilation. You will feel the joy of order, the peace of harmony, and the restfulness of a divinely accomplished plan. You will want what God wants, has always wanted; nothing more, nothing less. You will seek only to understand things as God Himself understands them, because He ordained them. You will repose in a supreme calm that no thing and no person can ever disturb.

Chapter
Four

# *Let the Faith keep your view of suffering in perspective*

In this loving approach to God, this blessed union with Him, there is no question of losing contact with human affairs, no tearing away from the world, no severing of ties that bind us to present life.

We have a word that defines all: the act most useful for a reasonable creature, his most important duty, and his most agreeable activity. It is the word *religare*, from which we derive the word *religion*.

Who will gainsay that the world admits religion to be the greatest, the loftiest, and the most characteristic of all things human? By religion, and by religion alone, man differs essentially from the brute creation. For science, art, education, industry, and social law are, in a sense or at least by their striking similarity, found to be applied in the habits of creatures inferior to man.

One thing, however, that we would be more than surprised to find in even the most perfect animal is religious action or even the mere caricature of it. No religious sentiment exists in any degree whatever among brutes, either by training or by instinct. This sentiment, as atheists themselves will admit, is therefore the only title to genuine nobility that man has.

What do we understand by the word *religare*?

*Religare* means to reunite, to bind. To bind what? Religion is the bond that unites man with God, the whole man with the infinite God. Why let anything trail behind? And what happens when this union is achieved? The human will is then united with the divine, everything human with everything divine.

### *All of your experiences endure*

My past may possibly have bitter memories of discord, of jealousies strongly expressed or suggested, memories of wearisome struggles, of moral and physical torments unillumined by the spirit, and whatnot. But I possess memories of tender love, of happiness, of profound and charming conversations, and of joyful achievements as well.

Ah, indeed! Why do we consider these excursions into the past as though they were visits to a cemetery? The past is not a tomb. Marble tombstones do not enshrine the sentiments and thoughts of those whose mortal remains we have entrusted to their keeping. So, too, does the soul of the past escape burial.

Our life may have turned from one sorrow to another, regrets may have followed joys and desires, the warm sentiments of yesterday may have grown cold and appear to be dead; but the spirit, the invisible elixir of vanished happier times, cannot thus be stifled. Once this gift has been given to us, it can never be taken away. The divine moments of the past continue to influence the days that the future has in store for us. There are moments that perfume a whole life; there are words that live on and on.

It is easy to say: everybody finds all of these things within himself. Let us delve deeper; let us go to the very roots.

Traditions have nourished heart and intelligence. The first impetus toward the good, the beautiful, toward the joys of human affections, has been transmitted to us by those who gave us birth, by our educators, by the familiar and friendly circle in which we have grown to adulthood. I give little heed to the fact that one encounters defects while making the first steps; things good and true are certainly interspersed with them. Nullify them? Never!

What cherished images people the sky of the years gone by! The distant visions of old fade away in a caressing glow. Let us bask in the matchless atmosphere of this distant background interwoven with our present environment. All is there, all continues, even that which seemed shattered long ago. Loyalty to our noble sentiments unifies, attracts, and reunites all these things. To scatter them is to break our heart; to gather them is to mend it. Learn, then, how to enjoy the indestructible love of things worth loving forever and preserve that which once was ours. Let nothing of all this be lost or vanish in frivolity or indifference.

To gather all this, and then to gather oneself is the great secret. But we dare not halt there. Reflection does not mean stagnation. We have neither the right nor the time to stop. This very moment — filled, enriched, and transfigured by the happiness we possessed in the past — we must now link with and weld to all that the future in its turn can offer us of happiness.

"Alas!" some say. "I see nothing really beautiful, nothing so happy in my past life. All that I hoped for has been denied me. All the castles I had built collapsed miserably one after another. Unescapable defeat dogged my efforts. Irreparable gaps have been torn in the circle of deepest affections. For me the future holds nothing but anxiety and fear. And you want to tell me about its fountain of joy!"

Exactly, because it is not built up on myth or chimera, but rather upon a most reasonable probability.

*Happiness may awaken in you at any time*

No one can say with absolute certainty, "There is no more happiness left for me on this earth." It is possible that one or another form of joy is definitely lost to you; but you never know when, under some other form or through some other means, joy, that thing so vast and at the same time so personal, will descend into your heart, even if it be only in passing. This is sufficient to awaken a flood of anticipated joys and cheer you onward. It suffices to permit trusting hope to enter upon the scene and crown the spiritualizing work of the memory.

If hope confined to the scope of your earthly destiny appears too stunted and limited, reach out to the end, even to the extreme limits of all hope, even to the goal of complete hope. Make it pass beyond the bounds of this world and lift you up to the infinite. There assured joy — complete, lasting joy — absolute joy awaits you.

What can prevent your turning the marvelous reflection of this promise upon your dimmed joys?

*You are already in eternity*

Do not dissociate life, this brief span of time, from the future life. What is time, and why should I separate it from eternity? Time is a succession of moments, and eternity is the endless "now." If we employ various terms to express that which after all is identical, such as duration, it is because we need this shade of difference to divide and classify everything which is inherent in our nature, which admits successive changes, and one change more striking than all others: death. We call this extraordinary change the passage from time to eternity. All that precedes this change we reckon in time; that which will follow this change pertains to eternity. But as a matter of fact, eternity began for us the very moment God first gave us life. Eternity engulfs, absorbs all time.

Consequently, the discouraging and depressing "All is ended," spoken to oneself and repeated in despair after an apparent loss — that is, after a momentary and temporary deprivation of favor or fortune — is as false as it is cruel. Ended? No! Changed? Yes, but not ended.

"But that is the same thing," says someone. Stop deceiving yourself. It is not the same thing.

What does "to end" mean? It means to pass from existence to nonexistence, to pass from something to nothing. "To change" means to remain the same in one respect and to become something different in another respect.

This is how death changes us. Thus, when we lose a beloved one through death, our relationship with that person is not ended, but simply changed. For the time being, we are deprived of the sight of this beloved person, and material communications between us are temporarily interrupted; but nothing is ended. Or rather, that which is ended is only the possibility of suffering for one another, of doing harm to one another. What remains is all the good we have mutually accomplished, all the love that united our hearts, and the hope of resuming these affectionate intimacies, devoid of all imperfections, in another world.

No matter what misfortunes may have befallen you, has your life, your destiny ended? No! Your conditions have merely changed and will change again, because nothing under the sun is permanent. Therefore, long live hope!

*You can find joy in what you hope for*

Hope is such a charming state. Even here on earth, the satisfaction found in hope is frequently greater than the satisfaction found in the realization of that hope. It has been said, "I prefer a present sorrow to a future one." A certain lady, when asked which was the happiest day of her life, answered, "The day before."

To hope is almost equivalent to immediate seizing. To have good reasons to hope, to have solid guarantees for the future possession of the object hoped for, is to enjoy happiness. The invalid who hopes to be cured because he feels himself well on the way to recovery; the youth who hopes for success in his examination because his tests have been satisfactory; the farmer who hopes for an abundant harvest because season and seedtime have been favorable: all of them are contented, delighted, because they have logical and solid reasons for their hope.

What is it that guarantees our supreme hope? What is it that commands us to acquire this optimistic state of hope? Religion.

God not only commands us not to be hopelessly depressed over the ills of life, but He also forbids us to rely upon the imperfect happiness that this life offers. He wants us to expect something more and better.

Why not enter immediately upon this enchanting perspective? Remove the frontier between the finite and the infinite. Unite them, because they fit so well together, because they form such a beautiful whole. This present life is the vestibule of eternity. May the door of communication always be an open passage that will allow you the free enjoyment of all the marvels you will find in the great beyond. The good work you are now undertaking, the child you are now raising, the friendship that you seal: all these are not merely for a day, just for the moment, for tomorrow, but for a future that knows no end. You are sowing for an imperishable harvest. Therefore, consign yourself to the charm of hope and await the fruits of the good you have sown during this earthly life.

### *Religion unites you with those in eternity*

Religion unites man with God as an atom of goodness with infinite goodness, the visible to the invisible. Religion also unites human persons whose feet tread tangible soil with the pure spirits who people the profound depths of the other world, with the souls who have already crossed the threshold of our prison.

The infidels who here might show their scorn make me smile. Were I to speak of occultism, telepathy, astrology, or mediums and ghosts, then sober freethinkers would take me seriously. But when I mention angels, saints, or the souls in Purgatory, I am charged with rehashing fables that are good enough only for old women and little children. The French Revolution also rejected the God of the Catholics in order to inaugurate their cult of a supreme being. And again, human pride will always seek to destroy the order established by a divine power, and substitute for it moldering foundations that originate in their own imagination.

An invisible world does exist. On this the impious and the pious frequently come to a perfect agreement. I am not speaking of a world full of wonders and mysteries, which although entirely material cannot be reached because our physical organs of sight lack sufficient refinement — namely, the realms of ether, the dizzy multitude of molecules and infinitesimal atoms, the domain of science in which one already finds a confusion and contradiction in the very narrow conceptions of skepticism, of rationalism, and of all other systems that seek to strike a blow at revealed truth, by explaining or denying all on the criterion of mere human comprehension.

I am now speaking of the world in which purely spiritual substances live and move. Their existence is affirmed by Revelation and proved by instinctive universal faith. Their participation in events is undeniable in the course of the history of mankind, so replete with surprises. Faith reveals it, and superstition confirms it in its own manner.

Spirits of light, the angels subject to God, are radiant agents in the execution of divine operations. Spirits of darkness, the rebellious, fallen angels, the demons, who are always active, are the detestable agents in the work of corruption.

*Superstition is misguided belief in the supernatural*

The ultraterrestrial influences solicit the human faculties. These interventions play their part as the mechanism of secondary causes in the earthly organization. How many subtle phenomena, bizarre coincidences, and unexpected and surprising results have turned up in even the most ordinary events? Science cannot account for all; chance explains nothing. We know that supposedly intelligent and well-informed persons will impute certain unlucky happenings to the dropping of a salt cellar, the breaking of a mirror, or meeting the number thirteen. Everybody knows that even in our own time, the booths of fortune tellers are patronized more than ever before.

What do all these manifestations of baseless credulity prove? What do these ridiculous practices manifest? They prove the existence of the need within us for the mysterious and the supernatural — legitimate tendencies, alas, diverted from their course. The mental state of the superstitious is simply a warping of the mentality of a believer. Yes, the brain and heart of man are drawn toward the supernatural as by a magnet. They are attracted by the mysterious. But his wicked pride, his imbecile pride, which insists upon feeling perfectly safe when there is a question of mediums and somnambulists, objects when there is a question of catechism or revelation.

That which renders those who sneeringly have been christened "strong-minded" most ridiculous is their belief in Satan and his satellites. Now, it is one of the favorite tricks of Satan to have his existence denied or disregarded by men. This is evident: we are always at the mercy of an enemy who, being invisible, is also considered absent or nonexistent.

This disregard or negation of the malevolent power of the evil spirits is all the more unfortunate, because the soul that labors under this delusion is afflicted with greater sadness. The gloomy soul is like those suffering from nervousness due to fatigue or privation, who cannot resist the attack of the disease. The gloomy soul, enfeebled, deprived of energy, becomes a prey to the clever suggestions of the Devil, always on the alert, and possibly succumbs to his temptation much more easily than the frivolous and dissipated soul.

*You can seek the intercession of those in Heaven*

Religion, which warns us against the dangers we run on account of devilish machinations, prepares our defense by setting us in contact with the benign inhabitants of the invisible world, with the good angels who guard us, with the saints whose powerful intercession protects us, and with our beloved departed, whom we are naturally inclined to beg for help and support. Religion establishes a communication between them — not through confused and equivocal practices without any guarantee, or impregnated with the poison of materialism and most frequently accompanied by deplorable psychological results, but through the soothing and refined aids that Christianity supplies: morality and piety.

If it is always helpful to bear in mind the possibility of this connection with benign spirits, is it not still more indispensable to do so in days of sorrow?

Does not the energy of great heroes, the resignation of victims, and the perseverance of the wise communicate itself to us as soon as we merely meditate upon their lives and their history? Does not that beloved one on whom I leaned, whose heart has ceased to beat at my side, still continue to be my guide and my support? Have I not been inspired and encouraged by merely falling back on intuition, just by thinking, "If he were here, under such circumstances, he would say this; he would do that"?

How persistently present he becomes through this practical habit. And at certain critical moments, do I not feel the exact advice of which I am in need whispered to me? Do I not also know that on my part, by means of my prayers, my sacrifices, and my virtuous acts, I can send to him beyond the tomb solace, and possibly the deliverance he is waiting for?

What is it that has authorized this exchange, that has approved these mystical conversations, and that has consecrated and blessed this sharing of sentiments, merits, and lights? Religion.

Chapter
Five

# See suffering as a precious gift

Suffering willingly borne before God, in His presence, under His eyes, while the soul is in union with Him "who is,"[9] in union with all the good emanating from His power, becomes supremely sweet and consoling. This enduring of affliction for religious motives is opposed to that consuming sorrow of rebels against God and of unbelievers. The benefits deriving from this kind of suffering become inestimable, if only we are able to say these words from the bottom of our heart, in every sad or merely painful circumstance of life, "My God, I believe, I hope, and I love You. I accept."

I suffer and I believe

*My God, I am convinced that this affliction was sent by You. You are the God of supreme justice and goodness, and therefore my suffering is just; it is useful; it is good.*

[9] Exod. 3:14.

I suffer and I hope

*My God, I await with joyful anticipation all the delights Your kindness can prepare for me in the days still allotted to me here on earth, and in the streams of eternal bliss that the ultimate entrance of my soul into Your supernal kingdom reserves for me.*

I suffer and I love You

*Indeed, my God, Your love being the very essence of the beautiful, of all happiness, and of all good, in loving You, I love all that deserves to be loved. And if I should love anything else besides You with a justifiable love, it is because that other thing comes from You, was made by You, and was given by You. Consequently, my love for that thing has Your benediction and approval.*

*This is the manner in which I love life and the things of life. Indeed, afflicted though I may be, I love life. If I love this life which is so replete with sorrows, even without being aware of it; if all that has life attracts me, and death makes me tremble and shudder; if the fact of being born, of entering life, has always been considered a joyful event among men, it is because You are the Life, O God, and in loving life, it is You, my God, whom I love. To live is to share in Your being, Your intelligence, Your beauty, and Your goodness, lavishly bestowed upon Your creation and possessed by Your essence in the mystery of infinity.*

*You should love life*

To receive life, to begin to live is the greatest earthly happiness. It is supreme happiness and, in its content, surpasses all others. Why? Because it is the only way to arrive at eternal union with God! A deep-rooted instinct, all too frequently smothered, which informs us of it, alone explains the abiding love of life anchored in the human heart. It explains the fear of death, because a terrible dread of possibly incurring the eternal privation of this union forcibly impresses upon our mind how terrible this change from our present condition might be. It explains — I do not say justifies — suicide, because the desperate gambler imagining wrongly that he has already lost the game of life (something that never happens) supposes that there is nothing left but to throw down his cards. It explains heroism by the very opposite reason. It explains all, and without it, nothing can be explained. Why love life, if it is only that which we see? How can we love life, if it only deceives us, crushes us, torments us, and kills us?

And withal, how can we help loving life and being thrilled with emotion and stirred with enthusiasm at the sight of life's splendors: the sacred wonders of its transmission; the ardor and joy of its fecundity; the masterpieces it produces and the geniuses it inspires?

*My God, how can I help loving life, which proceeds from You and which although shattered, troubled, degraded through our own fault, still retains so much of beauty that nothing can ever eradicate from the heart of man the force through which it clings to it.*

I suffer and I accept

*Indeed, my God, it is now easy for me to say, "I accept." I suffer and accept. By this I mean that I receive and take from Your hands the gift of pain that Your Providence prepares for me. Possibly the appearance of this gift is repugnant to my nature, but I recognize its essential propriety. It is accepted. I suffer, but resign myself.*

Those who thus resign themselves are neither cowards nor weaklings nor vanquished. René Bazin puts this triumphant dignity of resignation into beautiful relief when he says, "The intelligent man of faith who knows that nothing happens by chance, sums up his faith in the simple word *fiat*. He does not exhaust his strength; he renews it, rather, and though often obliged to change his course, he does not consider himself dispensed either from living or acting or continued hoping. Those who are resigned may be called conquerors of their trial. They yielded nothing to it that it did not seize. They are the ones whom pain does not make useless or wicked, and who up to the very end love something other than themselves."

My God, I believe, I hope, and I love You. I accept.

### *You should receive suffering as a gift*

It is quite necessary that we accept. Everyone must *espouse his suffering*, accept it even with joy, and unite himself with the will of Him who presents it and imposes it upon him. He must receive it, take it from His hands resolutely, as a command, and cheerfully as if it were a gift.

Of a truth, what we thus accept is really a gift. For pain has a purchasing value, one that is inestimable. By suffering — but suffering as we should — we purchase what cannot be bought at the price of gold. Pain is a marvelous coin, in exchange for which graces of every kind can be accorded to us for our own selves and for all to whom we wish well. If we understood the truth perfectly in this regard, or rather, if we could penetrate to the depths of this truth, we would acquire the desire for pain as a banker desires funds to increase his business in order to realize greater profits.

Delicate and haughty souls who might be confused at the commercialism of this theory permit me to forestall your indignation. You were about to say, "What? Would God (and it is He with whom we are now dealing) be a merchant who bargains with our afflictions? And should the nobility of suffering be degraded to the base level of commercialism?"

Pause a moment, if you please! What makes a deal vulgar? It is the mediocrity of the goods about which it turns. If this is the real reason for disdain, I am with you. I shall go still further, if you wish, and from disdain pass on to contempt, if by base commerce is meant dishonest commerce, commerce without conscience or loyalty.

But do not forget that the word *commerce* is also employed in a sense as lofty as the highest terms of philosophy. Do we not speak of commerce between two souls, between minds? I need not explain this here. If the commerce in which I am engaged involves an exchange of noble values, immaterial and superior to all values known here on earth; if, moreover, I conduct this exchange under the most loyal, the most scrupulously delicate, even generous conditions, I am devoting myself to something laudable and noble. There can be neither doubt nor dispute about this.

How could the dignity of the feudal lords justly claim and hold the respect of the common people? The lords and the common people entered into a commercial relationship, in a wider sense of the word. The princes waged war in order to ensure peace, the prosperity of their domains, and the comforts of life for their vassals; these, in return, tilled the soil, wove cloth, and wrought in iron to provide their rulers with the necessities of life. Both could either lower the standard of this interchange by a lack of consideration, or raise it by their probity. As a matter of fact, the former shed their blood along the way, while the latter contributed only their labor.

### *Suffering can be of great value*

In the sacred commerce that God permits a soul to carry on with Him, pain acquires a value of the highest order, in fact becomes the noblest of values. Suffering becomes a power. Those who suffer, those who are afflicted are the really wealthy people of this world. They are rich, but frequently they do not know how to spend.

Alas! We have capital at our disposal, but we ignore it and overlook its importance. We act like millionaires who perish and allow their families to perish in poverty for want of knowing what they own and how to use it intelligently.

Sorrow that is accepted in the spirit of faith is actually good fortune. Through it we acquire inestimable good for ourselves, for our friends, and for all in every kind of need.

How much charity could we do, if we did not allow any of the abundant "pain money" to be lost as it passes through our hands! If it is impossible to calculate the beneficent effect of a glass of water or a morsel of bread given to the unfortunate, how can one gauge the enduring value of a mite of suffering that is offered on behalf of a soul?

*God grants only what is good for you*

While asking for a temporal favor in return for having courageously accepted a certain affliction, we must be on guard, lest we frequently mistake the value of the temporal goods that excite our desires. Should we be mistaken, God in His honesty refuses to grant our request. This may astonish and at times scandalize us, because we do not understand exactly that the price we should pay for this trifle would be too much, and that God in His loyalty will substitute, without our being aware of it, something that is really far better than the object coveted.

God does not reject our sacrifices any more than He remains deaf to our prayers. Should we complain if, in remunerating and favoring us, His liberality reckons less with our wisdom than with His own?

# Chapter Six

# *Encourage others by suffering well*

Others to whom we, as victims of affliction, are bound by various and numerous obligations, corresponding with their relations toward us, can be divided into two classes: those who also happen to be the victims of some woe, and those who for the moment are free of sufferings. I say, "for the moment" because those who are smiling today are the afflicted of tomorrow or of yesterday.

A sensitive dramatic author has put this exquisite reflection on the lips of one of his characters: "Let us respect happiness almost as much as sorrow, my dear sister! It is so frail." Indeed, those who smile at life because, for the moment, life smiles at them form an unstable, constantly changing group. In contrast with those who are spared, behold those who weep with us, because for them also the present moment of life has ceased to smile.

We may be particularly attracted to the latter or to the former, but neither, under any condition, should be shunned. To avoid the unfortunate is to evade the duty of devotion and of fraternal helpfulness, to which we are bound throughout life in proportion to the means at our disposal. To avoid happy people is to give way to unwholesome suggestions of a sentiment that, although often well disguised, can always be detected, and can be comprised under the loathsome name *envy*.

Mark well! This sentiment can conceal itself under the mantle of charity. It often happens that afflicted people sympathize with persons more afflicted than themselves, finding in such emotion a sort of satisfaction. Why? Because sometimes — sometimes, not always — the sight of such unfortunates and contact with them evidently does not create an unbearable contrast with their own lot. Among such they feel a sense of equality, or perhaps even of superiority, and this sensation unconsciously soothes, satisfies, and relieves them. Pride, the curbing of which is the chief purpose of suffering, as a rule hardens itself against this. And humiliated pride, confronted with flourishing prosperity, turns to envy.

Thus it is easier to induce a person soured by misfortune to act kindly toward the poor than to make an affable gesture toward the fortunate. The wounded, bruised, broken heart instinctively turns toward the crushed and oppressed of life rather than toward the heroes of chance and fortune, because in such company, there is less pain to one's own sensitiveness and self-love.

Certainly, it is hard for one who has lost his fortune, who has failed to achieve success, to brush up against extravagance and glory. It is painful for a young lady whose heart has expanded in dreams of love and motherhood to realize that the freshness of her youth is gradually fading away with her hopes unrealized; or to pass beside betrothed and wedded couples whose radiant looks reveal mutual tenderness. It is hard for a widow who mourns the companion of her happiness, for the mother who has lost her children, to indulge in a visit with a woman happily surrounded by her loved ones. It is difficult to smile with tear-filled eyes, hard to look at merry marchers and dancers while one drags oneself along on two crutches.

It is more distressing, we believe, to avoid sullenly and defiantly the scenes of happiness and to cultivate only the company of persons who are quite as destitute, quite as unfortunate as we.

If laughter, gaiety, and health were to disappear from the face of the earth, all the afflicted and infirm would, we may be certain, experience an intensified distress, just as all the poor would become still more impoverished, if there were no rich people on earth.

The comparison that reason induces us to make between the easy, soft, and brilliant life of another, and our own painful, toilsome, cruel existence certainly carries with it a bitterness that often constitutes the worst element of our suffering. (Animals do not experience this. They do not "think" about their suffering. Hence their sufferings are infinitely less worthy of pity than those of man.)

However, reason guided by wisdom tells us that, if each and every one of our sorrows were accompanied by a swarm of similar misfortunes laying all humanity low; if not a single living being continued to possess the joys of which we have been deprived; if, finally, sorrow were so rampant on earth that no refuge for happiness were to be found, the result would be an incredible aggravation of suffering for each disinherited individual. Such a universal state of desolation would thwart the spirit of optimism, of all confident and courageous reaction to re-establish faith in a less frightful future in the hearts of all. Everybody would be crushed with despair, poisoned by the noxious fumes floating in from every point of the horizon.

*Bearing suffering well is inspiring*

On the other hand, beneficent emotions reach us from those homes in which happiness persists amid innumerable encompassing calamities. A radiance, a charm, emanates from these centers that react on bruised and aching hearts, unknown to them and despite their own will. Owing to some prevailing or approaching joy, these very people out of whose life all joy has disappeared renew life's struggle and resume their tasks. The sight of happiness compels the unfortunate to continue believing in it. The contagion of serene and joyous sentiments is felt despite one's will. Sternness and the chill of mature age melt before the warmth of youth. The vast economy of the universe preserves an equilibrium that otherwise would break under the terrible uniformity of suffering.

This is the reason why, even if we consider only our personal interests, we would do wrong to break all contacts with happy souls as soon as grief overtakes us. It would indicate both blundering stupidity and the lack of charity.

Let us not imagine that these happy people whom we now envy have no need of us. In some way or another, we can be of service to them. Have we the right to deny them what they might expect of us? If we owe them only an example of resignation and courage, are we authorized to deprive them of it?

∞

### *You must never let your suffering interfere with others' happiness*

Moreover, it is not a question of voluntarily and unnecessarily associating with those who smile and sing while we ourselves are in tears, and of taking part in the external manifestation of their joys while our own soul is ravaged with pain. But there is a simple rule that clearly points out the line of conduct to be followed by the afflicted: never, either by one's absence or presence, should anyone spoil or interfere with the complete or partial happiness others may be enjoying.

Therefore, away with all unjust reproaches, jealous recriminations, evil, brutal, perfidious insinuations, and useless lamentations, which weary, grieve, or exasperate those to whom they are addressed without actually bringing any consolation to those who utter them. Away with these stupid and unwarranted attitudes that cast a disturbing shadow on gatherings, entertainments, and other activities. Let there be none of these sullen absences that disconcert and disappoint friendly advances and cordial welcomes.

And if I cannot forego such attitudes, what will the result be for me? Antipathy and aversion, at least isolation and indifference. Before long a great void will encircle me; everyone will leave me to my own grief and ill-humor. No friendly hand-clasp, no commiseration of a sympathetic heart will be offered to warm my chilled feelings, revive my waning energies, temper the keenness of my regrets, and mellow the bitterness of my tears.

To remain interested in the happiness of others even while we ourselves are suffering, to respect and even to increase this happiness if possible, is the delicate blossom of one of the most beautiful flowers of suffering. Regard for the happiness of others is the wisdom of the unfortunate, just as regard for capital is the wealth of the poor.

Let those deprived of love, fortune, or glory bear nobly that portion of poverty which has been allotted to them. Their inferiority, whatever this may be, should not entice them either to hate or to murmur against their more favored brethren. The socialists of sorrow have never been consoled; it is only to the meek that possession of the land was promised.[10]

If to spoil the happiness of others on account of jealousy shows a foolish spitefulness, if to refrain from helping others who suffer because we happen to be peeved indicates a great dryness of heart, then to add deliberately to the suffering of others in the hope of relieving ourselves is supreme meanness. St. Paul says, "Bear ye one another's burdens,"[11] and not, "Unload your burdens upon the shoulders of others."

*How should I dare, O my God, to impose the weight of my own burden upon shoulders already bent beneath a crushing load, possibly much heavier than the one that is overwhelming me?*

*You cannot judge the intensity of others' sufferings*

But here we are facing a subtle problem. Do the invalids who surround me or whom I meet endure exactly the

[10]Matt. 5:4.

[11]Gal. 6:2.

same anguish I have? If their pain is not of the same nature as mine, is it nevertheless equally intense?

Everyone is inclined to imagine that he suffers more than his neighbor. The particular trial that befalls a man always seems the most terrible of all. One suffering from ill health maintains that illness is harder to bear than financial ruin, and would persuade another that, in the struggle against misery, a money wound is not fatal. The deceived lover will declare that the death of his beloved would have been easier to bear than her infidelity. He who has seen death enter his home will cry out, and with apparent reason, that no greater affliction could ever befall him. And this is not all. Of two persons enduring the identical affliction, one will always claim to be suffering more than the other, because of particular circumstances associated with his affliction or because of a difference in temperament and character.

It has been said that no two persons read the same book or look at the same picture: each sees that in which his own interest is centered, or which he is capable of appreciating. So, too, one may also say that no two persons ever endure exactly the same trial.

In the first place, who can calculate the degree of physical sensitiveness in each person? A kitchen maid, accustomed to handling cooking utensils, can pick up a glowing coal which has fallen from the oven and, without minding the burn, throw it back into the fire, whereas her mistress with manicured nails would endure great pain in doing the same thing.

Physical pain, at least, affects certain organisms less than others. Mental culture and civilization become the agents of increased sensitiveness. But the varying degree of courage with which individuals endure physical pain must also be taken into account. How, therefore, can one measure exactly the respective intensity of pain endured by a number of similar patients? It is impossible.

We can reason along the same line in regard to moral suffering. It varies indefinitely, in the same case, under the same circumstances, according to a thousand invisible peculiarities that one cannot appreciate.

What must be done, then, to solve the difficulty? Guard against the very irritating mania of presenting one's own afflictions as incomparably greater than those of others. Understand that this mania reveals a lack of tact, and at the same time shows poor judgment and an absence of charity. Avoid another tactless trait that consists in boasting about our own consolations and advantages in the presence of afflicted persons, knowing these persons to be deprived of them. It behooves everyone not to be self-centered, but to sympathize with the sorrows of others, and to have one's own sorrow serve only to advise us of the precautions to be taken in dressing certain wounds and the care to be observed in touching upon certain scars.

When we begin to view our own afflictions as a means of putting ourselves on an even footing with those who suffer, of understanding and comforting them, we possess the key that opens every heart and allows us to penetrate the sanctuary of peace and consolation. The divine art of healing and consoling belongs to those who themselves have experienced pain, and this to their own personal advantage. The better we understand pain, the greater the variety of pain we have experienced, the better shall we be able to soothe suffering. It is a painful and noble privilege.

In the mysterious idiom of pain, there exists an exchange of thoughts and sentiments that in any other language would be impossible and that brings to the soul unlooked-for riches and sweetness. At times it effects such a beautiful and harmonious understanding that those who experience it would never again wish to be without it. Someone has said, "Sorrow borne by two is almost joy." To carry the weight of sorrow with another invariably makes it feel less burdensome. We feel this alleviation in proportion to the earnestness with which we seek it. The least effort brings immediate results. Whatever power of abnegation we find in the invalid for whom we care quickly converts itself into a guide and help. The motives for patient endurance that we suggest react favorably on the afflicted soul when that soul plays the part of the consoler. The good that a soul consciously accomplishes in the successful revival of courage, in calming a tempest of despair, or in winning a smile back to lips that had lost their flexibility, develops into a feeling of intimate satisfaction carrying within itself both the sweetest balm and the purest recompense.

"Send forth your heart to suffer amid all ills," is the cry of the Samaritan of Rostand in her sudden apostolate. We may find it difficult to practice this superhuman precept incessantly, and since at every minute of the day and night, some one of our brothers is enduring misery in some form, we may have not a single minute to ourselves free of the thought of suffering. But this advice can be adapted in such a way as to avoid all bitterness, by preserving and increasing the fullness of its charitable efficacy. "Love thy neighbor and all he possesses will be thine. Thou takest it for thyself without depriving thy friend of it," says St. Bernard.[12]

We have observed that evil, far from existing by itself, is nothing other than the default, the lapse, the lack, or the absence of goodness. Let us, therefore, seek to fill this void and vacancy wherever we find it by doing good to our fellow men, by dispensing happiness to them. Thus shall we accomplish what St. Bernard suggests: "With all the power of love, let us take for ourselves all the joys of our neighbor! Thus shall we attain three excellent purposes: we shall fulfill in the most magnificent manner our task as consolers; we shall rid ourselves as completely as possible of our egotism; and we shall allow our soul to share in all the happiness that flourishes on earth."

[12] St. Bernard (1090-1153), Abbot of Clairvaux.

Chapter
Seven

# *Let your vocation help you in your suffering*

Following one's vocation is the first duty of every reasonable being. A person in the right place is not only infinitely more happy, but also renders infinitely greater service to mankind, than the one who is out of place. Vocation is recognized by two marks: attraction and fitness ratified by a call from God. It is clear that a piece of work is executed so much the better if the artist is attracted to it and is endowed with the skill required for its execution. Consequently general welfare, as well as the interest of the individual, demands that every man be in his proper place.

Except in certain very grave situations involving inescapable obligations, such as the care of one's family, or the tasks imposed by the precarious health or the slender means of close relatives, nothing justifies deserting the vocation to which one feels called. Pains, trials, or grief must not induce any to swerve from the chosen path, despite the temptation that at times sorely tries the sad, excited, or discouraged soul.

We have now reached the point of considering how a soul burdened with sorrow can bear it most worthily. The best, the only way to sustain one's strength and courage in suffering is to be faithful to one's vocation, no matter what the cost. Humanly speaking, this is the only way to help a soul find consolation.

"Console me? That is exactly what I do not want," will be the petulant rejoinder of one or another. Having lost what was loved above all else in this world, how can one admit that one can or wishes to be consoled?

We may as well admit the fact: one always finds a little consolation somewhere. Chateaubriand[13] once said that this is unfortunate. That depends. To be consoled by inferior things, by things worth less than those we have lost, is indeed a great misfortune. But to be consoled by superior means, with the aid of more elevated things, is not a misfortune.

If we could not be consoled in any manner or measure, if we were to remain forever in tears and crushed in a misfortune, ever feeling as we did when the calamity overtook us, then it would be better to die at once, lest

[13] François-René de Chateaubriand (1768-1848), French statesman and man of letters.

we become a burden to ourselves and to others. Such a case would surely be a great misfortune.

Hence everything depends upon the manner and the means we employ in consoling ourselves. Nothing is more pitiable, I am convinced, than to console oneself at the death of a dear one by adopting a dog or a cat, or by taking up gambling. Such things do happen. But to find consolation in straining all the energies of one's soul in the accomplishment of useful and beautiful works is no misfortune; rather, the contrary is true. To find consolation in work is infinitely nobler than to stagnate in the listlessness of sluggish melancholy.

"Work is the greatest diversion," was the observation of a plucky servant, who had had her worries, in speaking to her employer. This simple, good-hearted soul spoke truly, and undoubtedly was in accord with one of our modern philosophers, who drew this conclusion from his reflections on human life: "There is nothing better on earth for a man than to busy himself at his trade." To work at one's trade means to be faithful to vocational duties.

There is something great about a vocation. It is a joy and an honor, as well as an accomplishment. The entire being, physical and moral, finds its fullest expansion in it. The whole human race derives an advantage from the vocational achievements of each individual. He who makes a success of his vocation corresponds with the designs of God in his regard, and at the same time fulfills the needs of his own nature. All this results in an incomparable comfort in every action, and an imperishable serenity suffuses his whole life.

*Even in troubles, persevere in your vocation*

But this grand effect cannot be realized without effort and sacrifice. Even when it concerns a task absolutely suited to our capabilities, we must at times strive very hard and, above all, persevere. While occupied with tasks one knows himself able to accomplish, it is useless to heed certain moments of lassitude that take possession of heart, brain, and limbs. Success does not infallibly correspond with the effort; here as elsewhere, grief, impatiently borne, plays a discouraging role, tempts one to drop everything and whisper to oneself the fatal words: "What's the use?" With these words, the path to complete abandonment of every generous enterprise is opened; they present the perspective of a whole life unfolding itself in sluggish and sterile desolation.

All this changes if the soul courageously masters and invincibly consecrates itself to its vocation, which is to accomplish the work for which it is evidently suited. Despite all sorrows and woes, despite the irreparable calamities of a painful past, we must devote ourselves to our task or resume it. It makes no difference whether it be sublime or modest, brilliant or hidden. It is enough to know that it is the one that, under the circumstances, God demands of the soul. In its most humble manifestation, vocation means fidelity to the duties of our state of life.

There lies the refuge of a soul in sorrow, its asylum, its unfailing and most practical consolation. Conscientious work produces an extraordinary comfort in the soul; it banishes gloom from the heart, dissipates bitter thoughts, purifies the mind, and restores full vigor to the body. Let us repeat, "Work is the greatest *diversion*."

### *Your vocation helps you overcome boredom*

Have you ever reflected seriously on what it means to be bored, and on the futility of the means ordinarily employed to relieve oneself of *ennui*? What do we mean by being bored? The words are usually employed without an awareness of the great humiliation they imply: I am sick of myself! What an admission! I am bored with myself; I declare that I cannot satisfy myself. My personal resources are insufficient to distract or interest me, or they no longer exist. Sick of myself! What good will it do me to seek a change of environment, to hurry to new shows or new clubs? Wherever I go, I take myself along, and if I am displeased with myself, I carry my discomfiture along with me. There is only one way to stop this boredom, and that is to cease being annoyed with myself.

How can this be achieved? I must occupy myself with something interesting and useful. I must work, produce something, do my part. No one in all this world is utterly deprived of talent; and everybody should learn to know his resources and apply them. It matters not whether these faculties are more or less striking or profound, or bear on questions of greater or less gravity. What does matter is that we make ourselves useful at every turn and in every way, that we develop and share our natural talents, which hitherto have possibly been neglected even to the extent of being ignored. To seek them, to discover them in itself carries an element of interest. Once we have found them, it must become the urgent purpose to make them bear fruit even in the smallest and most modest spheres.

Who can describe the thrills of a soul that, although shaken by the storms of the most cruel trials, can devote itself entirely to the kind of life and to the occupations to which it feels itself unmistakably called? It would be a great wrong for that soul to repudiate its earthly mission just because sorrow has come upon it.

What a mistake it would be to drop the career for which one was destined, or the art one was called to cultivate! How wrong it would be to frustrate the good that might have been done to others, the beautiful end toward which they could be led, and to deprive oneself of the ennobling consolations through which the soul could soothe its own suffering.

### *The death of loved ones should not keep you from fulfilling your vocation*

Poor disheartened and disillusioned soul, if, through the death of a beloved one, you lose the charm and enthusiasm of former years, be certain that, in giving in to despondency and disillusionment, you are not taking the right means of honoring him whom you mourn in this world, nor of atoning for him in the other. If he could speak to you, he would doubtlessly tell you that his departure is no reason for you, laborer, to drop your tools; for you, musician, to interrupt your harmony; or for you, poet, savant, educator of the masses or of youth, to arrest the flight of your genius or your talent.

On the contrary, he would urge the supreme effort in the exercise of your faculties and encourage you to follow the aim that he knew inspired your soul during his lifetime. More than ever before, he should convince you of the necessity of making the gifts of God bear fruit within you and, while persuading you, reveal to you reasons so much the more decisive and peremptory because he would be judging these questions from the viewpoint of eternity.

Now, this supernatural viewpoint does not allow us to consider as insignificant the conditions under which the earthly existence of every individual unfolds itself. The contrary is true, because these conditions transmit their consequences into the world beyond — which for us will be richer and fuller in proportion to our natural development on earth when utilized to correspond perfectly with all that God has demanded and expected of us.

### *You must persevere in your vocation even when it frustrates you*

But here arises a terrible objection. How can I find solace for sorrow in my vocation when this sorrow is caused by the contradiction existing between the life I had hoped to live and the one to which I am presently condemned; if my very vocation has been frustrated and shattered; if I am enduring the martyrdom of finding myself out of place, constrained by occupations that are repugnant to all my faculties?

I concede this to be one of the worst trials any human being can be compelled to face. But after all, it is only a trial. In this, as in everything else, it is only necessary to see the hand of Providence and the manifestation of the will of God in order to regain peace and courage in accepting the sacrifice.

You say that you are not in the right place. Are you sure of that? Be not too hasty in giving this question a positive answer. Are you so sure that in a situation other than the one you now occupy, you would be more successful and satisfy your inclinations more completely?

Admitting that you are in the wrong place, permit us to ask how this happened. Is it your own mistake? Did you choose a position for which you were not qualified, because of a whim, shortsightedness, or misguided ambition? If so, correct your mistake at once, as long as there is still time for it. If it is already too late, do not think of your responsibilities and handicaps unless it is to deplore them once and for all before God, particularly if they imply your defiant resistance to His call and flagrant disobedience to His orders. Then, without stagnating in futile regrets, resolutely face your present situation and make the best of it.

Whether through your own fault or through force of circumstance, it is evident that you are compelled to live in conflict with your inclinations. The incumbent duties serve only to disgust you. Nonetheless, for you they are now duties, obligations sent by God. Considered in this light, they now become invested with a special beauty that cannot escape your notice. Herein lies the beginning of an attraction that should captivate your will even to the point of casting itself, charmed and conquered, into the delights of submission to God.

Besides this, or rather, in union with this exalted conception of your frustrated life, you have other resources. The vocation of no soul ever meets with complete defeat. In a life and occupation least suited to the tastes and capabilities of an individual, something is found to correspond with them. Whatever this may be, it should be seized, secured, and held with passionate grip. It may be a particular angle or point from which to consider the future. While thus reorientating your work, you yourself may derive from the present situation, imposed against your will, such an abundance of personal happiness and such usefulness for your neighbor as to astonish you.

### *Recreation and hobbies can refresh you*

Again, I admit that in the execution of functions that constitute your task, you may be frankly and absolutely apathetic. If so, do not hesitate to introduce timely hobbies — not, however, to the detriment of your duties, but to reanimate your spirit in occupations more suited to your taste, even if for a few moments only. To do this is neither a loss of time nor an expression of egotism. It is a means to protect and conserve your strength, your good humor, energy, and endurance for work. It is indispensable if, being of an active temperament, one is confined to a sedentary life, or being of a contemplative nature, one must deal chiefly with material things.

May I repeat: it is indispensable to devote some time to the demands of thwarted ambitions. This is a question of necessary recreation. In the etymological sense of the word, *recreation* means the renovation of life and strength through which one becomes much more capable of persisting in the fulfillment of disagreeable incumbent tasks. By the incidental satisfaction accorded to legitimate aspirations, one acquires that freshness, enthusiasm, and faculty of cheerful resilience without which no useful work can be accomplished, no devotedness can survive and attain its goal. These partial compensations, no doubt, will only imperfectly content the mind. They may even intensify a deep-seated regret over the loss of complete self-expression once known or imagined, but denied today. Still, what other substitute can sane reason offer?

Something else might be done. But it would not be reasonable, nor would it in the least conform with divine wisdom — namely, to destroy within yourself and utterly uproot those instincts, those unused talents, those repressed aspirations, and those faculties reduced to inaction, the cause of the desolation and despair in your frustrated life, in order no longer to suffer under their revolt.

Beware of that, poor soul, tortured and ill-resigned. This would be a crime.

*Your work can bear fruit in this life and in eternity*

A noble instinct, a beautiful natural gift, be it moral, intellectual or merely physical, although it be temporarily unemployed or even appear to be sterile, should never be smothered. For all you know, that gift may bring forth fruit tomorrow. If it is not productive in this world, it will certainly revive in the next, where the degree of happiness and glory to be enjoyed will be proportioned to the intensity and the nobility of our present aspirations. The more we have loved and desired love, truth, and beauty here on earth, the more shall we be satisfied with love, truth, and beauty in the realms above. The more ardent and glowing our heart has been, the greater our desire, whether attained or not, to employ usefully and fruitfully all the faculties we possess, so much the greater will be the joy we shall experience in our illumined soul and in the magnificence of our glorified bodies at the hour of resurrection to immortality.

You, all of you most unfortunate human beings, remain potentially happy. Be virtually and with all your strength what you cannot now actually be. The detachment counseled by Christian morality would be nothing more than a degrading mutilation of human greatness, did it seek to destroy in a soul all the blessed instincts to which a crucified life denies satisfaction. Christian detachment has only one purpose: to judge all from a supernatural point of view. This viewpoint envelops and includes the natural perspective; it does not annihilate it, but surpasses it. Christian detachment consists in cultivating within oneself the desire for good in all its forms, then to receive and accept with equal joy the decrees of Providence, whether they deny or grant the immediate realizations of one's desires. The realizations in the next life will be the more splendid, the greater our privations endured with a supernatural motive have been in this life, and, above all, the more complete their acceptation has been.

So expand your lungs and your soul. Breathe, live, assert yourself. Truth is with those who say, "Yes!"; who believe and resign themselves. Error is with those who say, "No!"; who shirk and rebel. God revealed Himself in the burning bush to Moses, saying, "I am who am."[14]

[14]Exod. 3:14.

Satan, however, can repeat the words in which the poet describes him: "I am the one who always denies."

To live with a worthy motive as great as possible here on earth, to enjoy and achieve with the most complete satisfaction what God authorizes and permits, on the one hand; and on the other, with equal enthusiasm, to reserve this realization for the brilliant dawn "of the day that knows no end," if God so deems best — this is the plan by which to conquer all the demoralization and regrettable decay into which our sorrow impatiently borne causes us to fall.

No matter what the nature of the blow that has felled us may be, we must rise again, brace up, take new courage, and march on.

*Sophia Institute Press®*

# Sophia Institute

Sophia Institute is a nonprofit institution that seeks to nurture the spiritual, moral, and cultural life of souls and to spread the Gospel of Christ in conformity with the authentic teachings of the Roman Catholic Church.

Sophia Institute Press fulfills this mission by offering translations, reprints, and new publications that afford readers a rich source of the enduring wisdom of mankind.

Sophia Institute also operates two popular online Catholic resources: CrisisMagazine.com and CatholicExchange.com.

*Crisis Magazine* provides insightful cultural analysis that arms readers with the arguments necessary for navigating the ideological and theological minefields of the day. *Catholic Exchange* provides world news from a Catholic perspective as well as daily devotionals and articles that will help you to grow in holiness and live a life consistent with the teachings of the Church.

In 2013, Sophia Institute launched Sophia Institute for Teachers to renew and rebuild Catholic culture through service to Catholic education. With the goal of nurturing the spiritual, moral, and cultural life of souls, and an abiding respect for the role and work of teachers, we strive to provide materials and programs that are at once enlightening to the mind and ennobling to the heart; faithful and complete, as well as useful and practical.

Sophia Institute gratefully recognizes the Solidarity Association for preserving and encouraging the growth of our apostolate over the course of many years. Without their generous and timely support, this book would not be in your hands.

www.SophiaInstitute.com
www.CatholicExchange.com
www.CrisisMagazine.com
www.SophiaInstituteforTeachers.org

Sophia Institute Press® is a registered trademark of Sophia Institute.
Sophia Institute is a tax-exempt institution as defined by the Internal Revenue Code, Section 501(c)(3). Tax I.D. 22-2548708.